T0016988

FOR _____

IN MEMORY OF _____

FROM _____

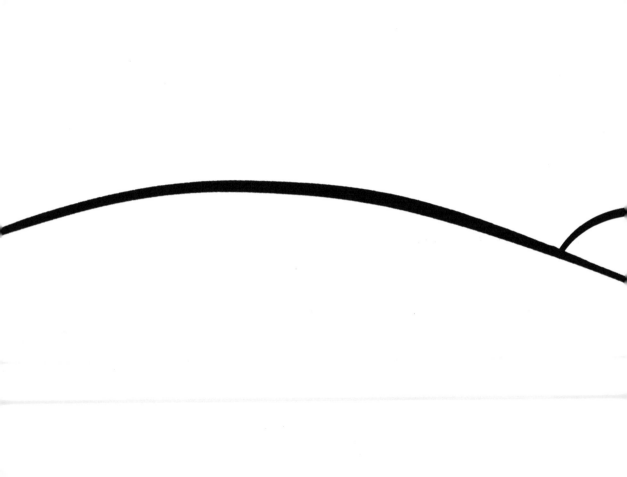

WHEN YOU LOSE A BELOVED PET

WRITTEN &
ILLUSTRATED BY
JOANNE FINK

WHEN YOU LOSE A BELOVED PET

CompanionHouse Books™ is an imprint of Fox Chapel Publishing.

Project Team
Managing Editor: Gretchen Bacon
Copy Editor: Christa Oestreich
Designer: David Fisk

ISBN 978-1-62008-430-4

Library of Congress Control Number: 2023934928

Fox Chapel Publishing | 903 Square Street | Mount Joy, PA 17552

We are always looking for talented authors. To submit an idea, please send a brief inquiry to acquisitions@foxchapelpublishing.com.

Printed and bound in China
2 4 6 8 10 9 7 5 3 1

DEDICATION

THIS BOOK IS DEDICATED
TO EVERYONE WHO IS
MOURNING THE LOSS
OF A BELOVED PET

FOREWORD

Joanne Fink has written this lovely and sensitive book to help people who have suffered the loss of a beloved pet. Because we share our day-to-day lives with them, we may have an even closer bond with our pets than with some human family members. Our pets do not judge us or argue with us; they offer unconditional love and companionship. They do not care about our social status, appearance, political views, or finances. They simply love and accept us. They can be our refuge in a difficult, stressful world, our support, and our connection to nature and to other people.

As a pet parent and veterinarian of many years who now deals exclusively with end-of-life care and home euthanasia, I know that losing a cherished pet can be incredibly difficult. This book illustrates that losing a beloved pet can trigger difficult emotions. Our pet's absence may remind us of other losses, alter our daily routines, leave us lonely, or cause feelings of guilt surrounding treatment choices. This book can help you remember the loving home you gave your pet and appreciate all that they gave you in return.

There is no timetable for grief. Give yourself permission to grieve as long as you need to. This book can be part of your healing process. Seek out people who understand what a significant loss this is for you, whether by talking to individuals, going to counseling, or connecting through online groups. Many are comforted by religion or thoughts of their pet in a happy place with others who passed before. Focus on the time you had together, rather than on the end of your pet's life.

When You Lose a Beloved Pet will help you celebrate the bond you shared so that you can move through grief into gratitude for all that your friend brought to your life. This book will bring you comfort and help you along your journey.

Wishing you peace and healing,

Sharon Sernik, DVM
Journey's End Home Euthanasia Service, Merrimack, NH
www.the-journeys-end.com

INTRODUCTION

♡

When You Lose a Beloved Pet is a companion to *When You Lose Someone You Love*, the book I wrote after my husband died unexpectedly in 2011. On my grief journey I discovered that most people aren't comfortable talking about loss—and although people care, they often don't know how to provide meaningful support for the bereaved. To honor Andy's memory, I became a grief educator, and began using my creative gifts to help others who are grieving the loss of a loved one.

As a lifelong animal lover, I know pets hold a special place in our hearts. In addition to dogs, cats, hamsters, and guinea pigs, throughout our 33 years together Andy and I had iguanas, saltwater fish, an African grey parrot, a ball python, and Elmo, our red-footed tortoise.

Although I cherished our many pets and remember them fondly, I haven't lost a pet since our cat Oliver died in 2009. When I decided to write this book, I wanted input from others who have lost pets and immediately reached out to one of the wisest people I know—my lifelong friend, Penny Tsaltas Lisk. I am deeply grateful to Penny for sharing the grief she experienced after her beloved cats, Cleo and Greta, and more recently her English Setter, Daisy, died.

A few weeks after I started this project, my daughter's four-year-old dog died unexpectedly. I live 1,800 miles away, only met Mr Bush a couple of times, and was astonished at how sad I felt. My heart goes out to my daughter, Samantha Trattner, and her significant other, Jon Cox, on their loss. Several of the pages in this book are a result of listening to them process their grief. The loss of a family member—whether a person or pet—is extremely hard, and I hope that this book will bring comfort to everyone who is grieving.

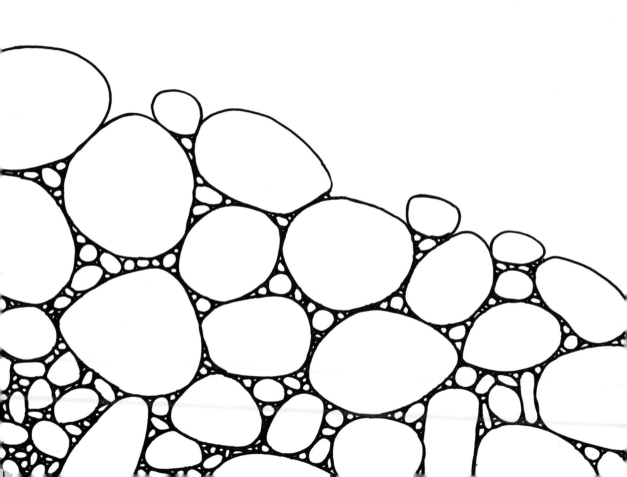

The "Forever in Our Hearts" illustration on the next page holds the names of pets that were important to me or to someone I love. There are several blank spaces for you to write the names of pets that have touched your life.

May the memories of happy times you spent together bring you comfort as you remember your beloved pet.

With sympathy on your loss,

Joanne Fink

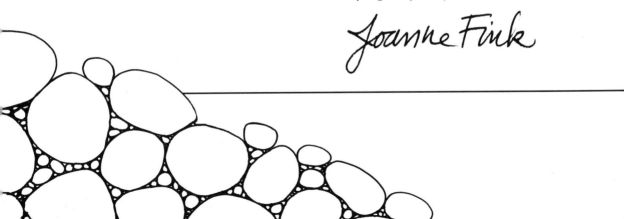

MR BUSH

Alexander

PRINCESS   MILO   OLIVER   WHEATINA   BUTTON

TINA   KANE   NOELY   Cleo   Greta   ZING   SUMMER   ANGEL   NALA

RUSTY   BONGO   RASHI   BAGEL   DAISY   CODY   CASH   KATO   ALI

SOPHIE   OLIVE   ARTHUR   DC   MAX   MOLLY   SNICKERS

HERCULES   PAUSE   RUDY   MIMI   TSUMI

SALVADORE   BO   BRANDY   TIKVAH   CASEY

BOY   MURPHY

ALLIE   YOYO   STRAWBERRY   DOZER   JADE   LA   SHAYNA

ALFIE   TYSON   MOLLY ANN   TOBY   PUNIM

BAXTER   TEDDY BEAR   ARBY   HARI'BO   STORMY

NIBBLES   CHARLIE   PHOEBE   GoGo   GIGI   CHECKER   ELIZA

CRICKET   BUZZY   BISCUIT   RALPH   FLUFF   HEIDI   MARIPOSA

SHADOW

Forever
IN OUR HEARTS

KUGEL · REDD · BAILEY · KATHRYN · ZURI · WITTEN · ANDY · FRIDAY · JELLICO · MISSY · POOKIE · TINKERBELL · ROSIE · DAGNY · DREIDEL · ELWOOD · RAFI · MIKA · SUGAR · DJ · BAT CAT · LULU · MOJO · YOGI · OREO · FRED · TAR · MAZEL · HOWIE · GIZMO · ELMO · THOR · BENNY · SPIRIT · CLYDE · COOKIE · WHISKERS · MAJOR · SHOFAR · CHLOE · HONEY · REX · MUFFIN · LITTLE BIT · SWEETIE · SHADY · LACE · PATCHES · TOJO · SHMEENY · SHAN · B.J. · GILLIGAN · JAKE · MADISON · ENKINS · TYLER · NICOLETTE · CHICO · LATCHKEY CAT · MATZAH BALL · ARCHIE · DIESEL · BURT · SKIDMORE · TIGER · MR. KITTY · VELVET · BYRON · CARLISLE · PARIS

WHEN YOU LOSE A BELOVED PET

THERE'S A HOLE IN YOUR HEART THAT NOTHING CAN FILL

YOU MISS THE UNCONDITIONAL *Love* YOUR PET PROVIDED...

AND THEIR CONSTANT

presence

IN YOUR LIFE

SOMETIMES
IT CAN BE HARD
TO GET THROUGH THE DAY

WITHOUT CRYING

WHEN YOUR PET DIES
YOU MAY EXPERIENCE
THE PROFOUND

SADNESS
OF GRIEF

YOU MISS THE THINGS YOU

USED TO DO TOGETHER
AND YOU MISS THE
DEEP BOND
YOU SHARED

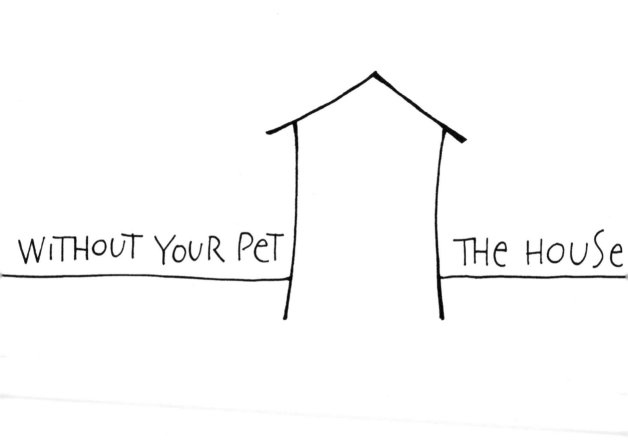

WITHOUT YOUR PET   THE HOUSE

CAN SEEM REALLY Quiet & REALLY EMPTY

SOMETIMES THE QUIET

CAN BE

OVERWHELMING

WHEN YOU LOSE A BELOVED PET

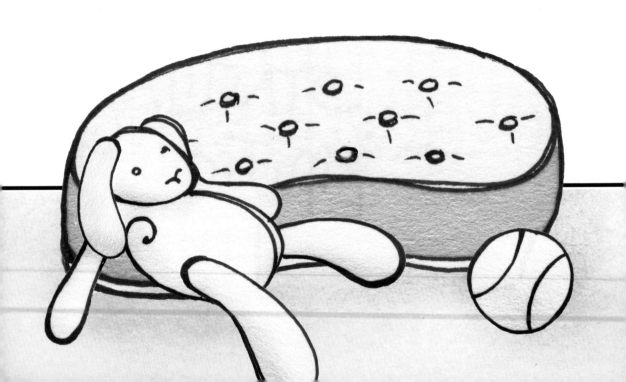

YOU DON'T KNOW WHAT TO DO WITH THEIR THINGS

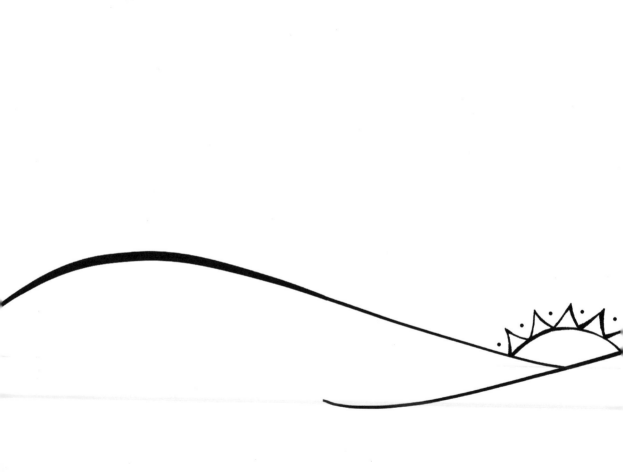

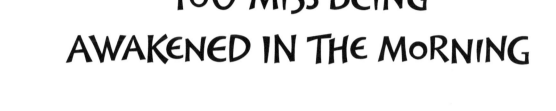

YOU MISS BEING
AWAKENED IN THE MORNING

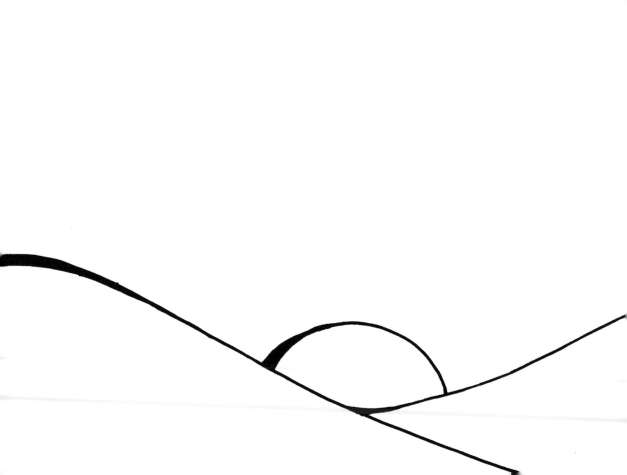

AND WELCOMED
BY YOUR BELOVED PET
WHEN YOU COME HOME

AND THE FUN THINGS YOU DID TOGETHER

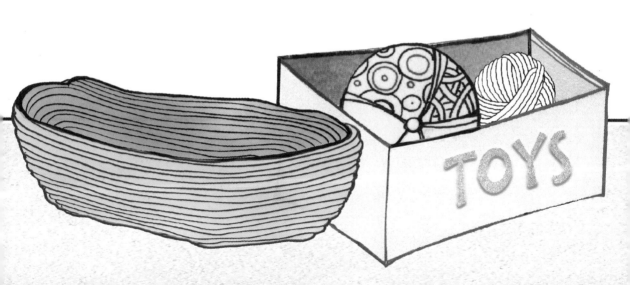

YOU MISS YOUR PET'S

PHYSICAL PRESENCE

AND THE SOUNDS THEY MADE

AND YOU MISS
HAVING NEW PET STORIES
AND PICTURES TO SHARE

YOU FEEL off BALANCE

AND IT CAN TAKE
A LONG TIME TO
ReGAIN
YOUR
Equilibrium

LOSING A BELOVED PET IS
HEART
BREAKING

IT CAN BE HARD
TO TALK ABOUT
YOUR LOSS...

ESPECIALLY WITH THOSE
WHO DON'T HAVE PETS...

OR THOSE
YOU THINK

CAN'T POSSIBLY

UNDERSTAND

WHAT YOU ARE
GOING THROUGH

OR WHAT A BI

G LOSS THIS IS

LOSING A BELOVED PET
IS LOSING A MEMBER OF

Your Family

AND CAN HURT AS MUCH AS
LOSING A PERSON YOU LOVE

SUNDAY	MONDAY	TUESDAY	WEDNESDAY	THURSDAY	FRIDAY	SATURDAY
♡	1	2	3	4	5	6
7	8	9	10	11	12	13
14	15	16	17	18	19	20
21	22	23	24	25	26	27
28	29	30	31	○	◑	☆ ◷

WHEN YOU LOSE A PET YOU LOVE,
YOUR DAILY SCHEDULE

CHANGES

IT CAN TAKE A LONG TIME
TO ADJUST TO THE FACT

THAT YOUR
BELOVED PET IS GONE.

YOU MAY FEEL MORE

VULNERABLE

WITHOUT YOUR PET

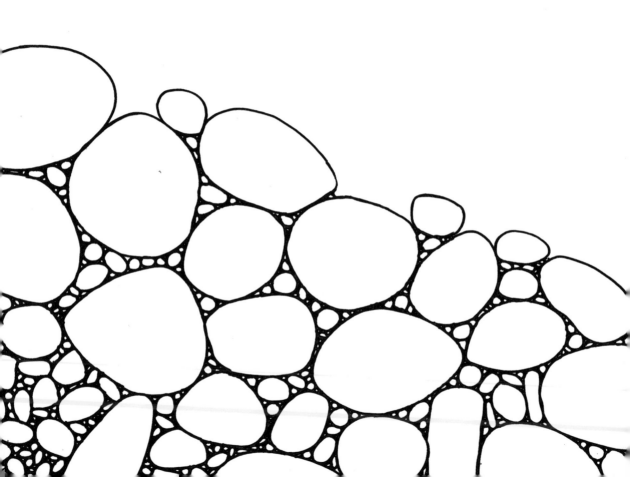

THE LOSS iS eSPeCiaLLY HARD

iF YOU LiVE

ALONE

OR IF YOU
DON'T KNOW
WHAT HAPPENED
TO THEM...

THE LOSS OF YOUR PET
MAY REMIND YOU
OF OTHER LOSSES
YOU'VE EXPERIENCED

THERE ARE TIMES YOU MAY

FEEL UNEXPECTEDLY SAD...

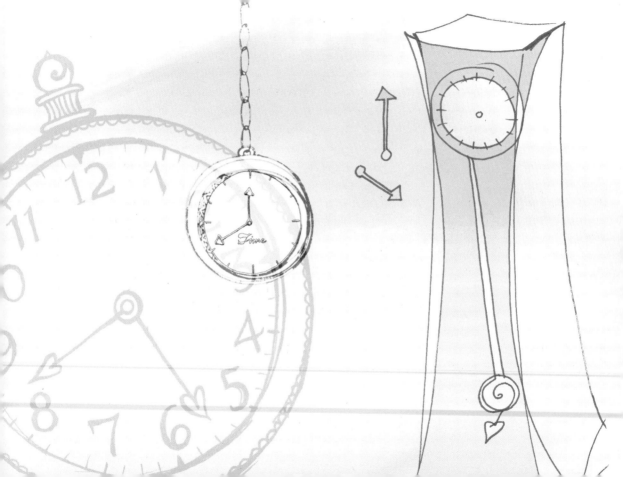

SOMETIMES
YOU WISH
YOU COULD
TURN THE
CLOCK BACK...

SOMETIMES YOU THINK YOU SEE YOUR PET...

AND YOUR HEART   SKIPS A BEAT

WHEN YOU LOSE
A BELOVED PET

YOU MAY FEEL GUILTY
THAT YOU WEREN'T
ABLE TO SAVE THEM...

YOU WISH YOU
COULD HAVE HAD
MORE TIME TOGETHER

HOLIDAYS AND SPECIAL OCCASIONS
CAN BE VERY HARD
WITHOUT YOUR PET

THOUGH YOU KNEW THIS DAY WOULD EVENTUALLY COME...

IT'S REALLY HARD TO SAY

Goodbye

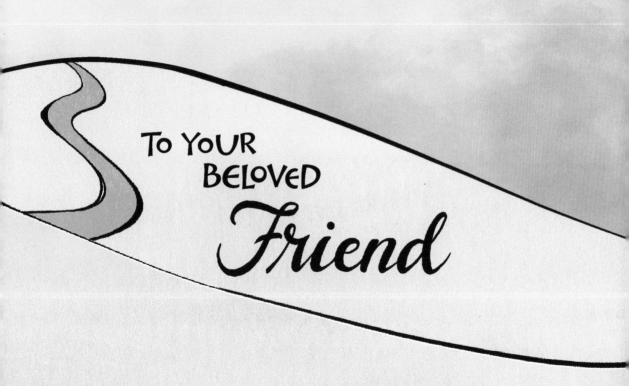

TO YOUR
BELOVED
Friend

YOU. JUST. MISS. THEM.
AND WISH THEY
WERE STILL HERE...

YOU WONDER
IF GETTING
ANOTHER PET
WOULD HELP HEAL
YOUR HEART

GRIEF

IS THE PRICE

WE PAY FOR

LOVE

EVEN ON YOUR
SADDEST DAYS

YOU ARE GRATEFUL FOR
THE TIME YOU HAD
together

THE SPECIAL RELATIONSHIP YOU HAD WITH YOUR PET

MAY MAKE YOU WANT
THAT KIND OF

You **Remember**

WHEN YOU FIRST GOT YOUR PET...

AND THE

Joy

THEY BROUGHT INTO YOUR LIFE

Remembering
WITH
L♥VE

YOU LOOK FOR WAYS TO KEEP THEIR MEMORY ALIVE

YOU KNOW YOU WILL
ALWAYS MISS THEM...

AND THAT THEY WILL
ALWAYS HAVE A SPECIAL PLACE
IN YOUR HEART

AND THE BEAUTIFUL MOMENTS
YOU HAD TOGETHER

AT THE

Rainbow

BRIDGE

LIVE IN YOUR HEART

Forever

ACKNOWLEDGEMENTS

I am grateful to Alan Giagnocavo, Dave Miller, Gretchen Bacon, and the entire Fox Chapel/CompanionHouse Books publishing team for all their support.

My deepest appreciation to Penny Tsaltas Lisk for her invaluable input and design suggestions, and to Jonathan Trattner for reading and commenting on multiple versions of the book. Special thanks to my friends Sandi Atkinson, Maura Cooper, Mary Anne Fellows, Philip Fleet, Jill Goldsmith, Pete Johnson, Lara Parish, Reeva Shaffer, and Bonnie Srolovitz for their careful review and thoughtful comments.

I also want to thank those who shared their pet loss journeys and provided input on the book, especially Ann Klahr, Arianne Bahnson, Dana Kaplan, Darlyne Biggerstaff, Ellen Gliksman, Emily Chesick, Goldie Milgrim, Gordon Fink, Grace Chan, Jamie Torres, Julie Ager, Kathleen Hill, Kathleen Hooker, Ketra Oberlander, Tammy Browning-Smith, and Terri Misek.

My heartfelt thanks to my friend, Dr. Sharon Sernik, of Journey's End Home Euthanasia Service in Merrimack, NH, for writing the foreword. Sharon read every draft, and the suggestions she offered made *When You Lose a Beloved Pet* a better book.

And lastly, my appreciation for everyone who, as Sharon puts it, "did the best they could out of love for their pet" when making the difficult decision to say goodbye. I hope this book will bring you comfort as you remember your beloved pet.

Love is Eternal

Additional copies of
When You Lose a Beloved Pet
&
When You Lose Someone You Love

are available through

www.FoxChapelPublishing.com
www.WhenYouLoseSomeone.com